Forward by Deborah Grey, O.C. M.P. (Retired)

# Ready or Not, the Bridegroom is Coming!

## Fuel Up and Get Ready to Ride

LINDA RYTKONEN

PRESS

# Special Thanks

All praise, glory, and honour to God.
For without You, Lord, I have no story to write.
Thank You for Your guidance.

My husband, Peter—thank you for
igniting my passion,
and thank you for persevering through hurdles and
challenges in teaching me to ride a motorcycle.

And to our daughters, Jessica and Jennifer,
thank you for your love and faith.

My mentor and editor, Vicki Crompton—thank you
for your support, prayers, great questions,
and keen insights.

## A Blessing for the Reader

May you come to know God's love

in a deeper and fuller capacity

until He comes again in glory!


May God give you a heart's desire to

love and serve Him all of your days.


May your relationship with God

be a two-way relationship where you

converse with Him regularly throughout your day.


And may God grow in you the Fruit of the Spirit

which is:

love, joy, peace, patience, kindness, goodness,

faithfulness, gentleness, and self-control.

And may this book encourage
you on your journey in view
of eternity ♥ Linda

# Forward

I have enjoyed Linda's stories about learning to ride a motorcycle in what was once a man's sport. I know, firsthand, what it is like to enter a similar arena as the first Reform Member of Parliament; one of very few women in what was, and is, very much a man's world. I also have been riding a motorcycle since 1968, when you would hardly ever see a woman "manning" a motorcycle!

Linda has provided a great take-off point from which to view the opportunities and challenges each of us will face before the cry is heard, "The Bridegroom is here!"

**Deborah Grey**, O.C. M.P. (Retired)

# Contents

# CHAPTER ONE

# Are You Ready to Ride?

**"A** *re you ready to ride?"* This is the question my husband, Peter, asks me before we head out on our sport bikes for yet another adventure.

In the early days of learning how to ride a motorcycle, my knees would knock, my heart would race, and my hands would get cold and clammy as I tried to muster enough courage to squeak out an affirmative answer. "I think so ...."

You would think that Peter was asking me if I was ready to cliff dive or bungee jump or swim with the sharks. Learning to ride a motorcycle, for me, was similar to engaging in an extreme sport which was filled with peril, should I choose to join him.

Maybe your response to the same question might be, "I was born ready—bring it on!!" But more than likely you are like me, filled with fear and trepidation; you want to respond, "Don't you have a buddy who is willing to ride with you?"

Having a certain degree of anxiety about being ready is a good thing if it leads us to action. If you know what you need to be ready for, by when, and what is required, you can alleviate the anxiety to some degree. There are many areas in our lives where we face the challenge of being ready. The following are some examples from my life:

"Are you ready to go to your new school?" The first day in a new school could be exciting and terrifying at the same time. As a child, I was timid and shy and meeting new friends was not easy for me. I was lucky when my older sister had me under her wing and did the social networking for me. We moved often and I attended seven schools in 12 years. With each move, I was able to become more comfortable with change and adapting to new situations. These experiences have benefited me as I developed new relationships, changed jobs, or moved to new locations as an adult.

"Are you ready for your wedding?" Preparing for a wedding is more than simply preparing for a ceremony. Sure there are plenty of details to be taken care of, such as choosing the venue and the minister, and putting together the list of invitees. Getting married can be one of the most exciting events in a person's life and it can also bring about the greatest anxiety! I was certainly ready to be married, set up a home, and have a family, however, the future was full of unknowns and I was hopeful, at best, that I was marrying the right person. I wanted to marry a man who would be a supportive and loving husband, a good provider, and a loving father for our children.

"Are you ready to have your baby?" When I was pregnant with our first child, I was excited about bringing the baby home. I had wallpapered the baby's nursery with adorable baby fawns and bunny rabbits and outfitted the room with a crib, dresser, and change table. I was well informed about what to expect in the hospital and my doctor was very encouraging. However, I was terrified at the thought of what I would experience in giving birth. I was hoping for a normal delivery but I knew there was potential for a difficult birth and I might have to deal with issues regarding the baby's health. Thankfully our two daughters were born healthy and without too much difficulty. Parenting comes with many opportunities and challenges, and requires preparation and planning in order to be successful. I wasn't always prepared or ready for each stage of development, but thankfully I had many chances to do it better.

"Are you ready to say good-bye?" My first husband, Howard, died suddenly after six short years of marriage. There is little anyone can do to prepare for such a great loss emotionally, but we have the responsibility of preparing for death in order to ensure our family is taken care of legally and financially. This preparation is often tragically neglected, as was the case in our marriage.

"Are you ready to form a new family?" This next stage of my life brought more excitement and anxiety as Peter married into our ready-made family with the girls entering their teen years. Peter needed to be ready to be a husband and a father as he stepped into this marriage covenant and I needed to be prepared to share my life with my new husband, as well as share the parenting role once again.

"Are you ready to learn a new skill?" Life changes are not the only areas in which we need to be prepared. If you become interested in learning to play an instrument you don't simply pick up a guitar and expect to be proficient at playing. It takes discipline, practice, and courage to perform. The same goes for developing skill in sports or sciences or technology.

"How about travel? Are you ready for your cruise to Alaska?" Recently our family had the opportunity to board the MS Ryndam for a family reunion vacation. We visited the ports of Vancouver, Juneau, Skagway, and Ketchikan. We had a year to think about and prepare for the trip. It was exciting to plan the details. As the time approached, however, anxiety kicked in and I started to worry that I might forget something, or get ill, or even get stuck in traffic and miss the boat!

There are those who seem to thrive on last-minute pressure. They act as though there is no need to worry and everything will take care of itself. They may ask others for help when they suddenly realize there isn't enough time left to be prepared. This may work out, but it is risky because there are often steps they need to do for themselves in order to be ready.

Recently I came across a parable in the Bible that caught my attention. Actually, it more than caught my attention—it gave me cause for concern, because it was a message that came with a warning about being ready.

The parable is titled, "The Parable of the Ten Virgins," or "The Parable of the Ten Bridesmaids," depending on the version you read. It is recorded in the book of Matthew, chapter 25. In the parable, Jesus shares a story about the coming kingdom of God and the importance of being ready:

### Matthew 25:1-13

### The Parable of the Ten Virgins

*¹At that time the kingdom of heaven will be like ten virgins who took their lamps and went out to meet the bridegroom. ² Five of them were foolish and five were wise. ³ The foolish ones took their lamps but did not take any oil with them. ⁴ The wise ones, however, took oil in jars along with their lamps. ⁵ The bridegroom was a long time in coming, and they all became drowsy and fell asleep.*

*⁶ At midnight the cry rang out: "Here's the bride-groom! Come out to meet him!"*

*⁷ Then all the virgins woke up and trimmed their lamps. ⁸ The foolish ones said to the wise, "Give us some of your oil; our lamps are going out."*

*⁹ "No," they replied, "there may not be enough for both us and you. Instead, go to those who sell oil and buy some for yourselves."*

*¹⁰ But while they were on their way to buy the oil, the bridegroom arrived. The virgins who were ready went in with him to the wedding banquet. And the door was shut.*

*¹¹ Later the others also came. "Lord, Lord," they said, "open the door for us!"*

*¹² But he replied, "Truly I tell you, I don't know you."*

*¹³ Therefore keep watch, because you do not know the day or the hour.*

While this message appears to be addressed to women, we find in the book of Luke that Jesus shares a similar parable to warn men to keep their lamps burning and to be ready and waiting for His return.

Let's have a look at the warning Jesus offers to men:

### Luke 12:35-40

*[35] Be dressed ready for service and keep your lamps burning, [36] like servants waiting for their master to return from a wedding banquet, so that when he comes and knocks they can immediately open the door for him. [37] It will be good for those servants whose master finds them watching when he comes. Truly I tell you, he will dress himself to serve, will have them recline at the table and will come and wait on them. [38] It will be good for those servants whose master finds them ready, even if he comes in the middle of the night or toward daybreak. [39] But understand this: If the owner of the house had known at what hour the thief was coming, he would not have let his house be broken into. [40] You also must be ready, because the Son of Man will come at an hour when you do not expect him.*

Jesus had a profound understanding of God, and like the rabbis of His time, He used simple word-pictures, called parables, to teach who God is and what His kingdom or reign is like. Jesus used images and characters taken from everyday life to illustrate His message. This was His most common way of teaching.

His stories appealed to the young and old, poor and rich, and to the learned and unlearned. Over a third of the Gospels contain parables told by Jesus. He loved to use illustrations to reach the hearts of His listeners through their imaginations. These stories challenged the minds of His listeners to discover anew what God is like and moved their hearts to make a response to God's love and truth.

Jesus' parables have a double meaning. First is the literal meaning, apparent to anyone who has experience with the subject matter. Beyond the literal interpretation lies a deeper meaning—a beneath-the-surface lesson about God's truth and His kingdom.

Jesus told His disciples not everyone would understand His parables:

*Luke 8:10*

*[10] He said, "The knowledge of the secrets of the kingdom of God has been given to you, but to others I speak in parables, so that,*

*'though seeing, they may not see;*

*though hearing, they may not understand.'"*

Did Jesus mean to say He was deliberately confusing His listeners? Likely not: Jesus was speaking from experience. He was aware that some who heard His parables refused to understand them because their hearts were closed to what He was saying. They had already made up their minds not to believe. God can only reveal the secrets of His kingdom to the humble and trusting person who acknowledges the need for God and for His truth. The parables of Jesus will enlighten us if we approach them with an open mind and heart, ready to let them challenge us. If we approach them with the conviction that we already know the answer, then we, too, may look but not see, listen but not hear or understand.

As Jesus' parables are mysteries meant to be revealed to believers in Christ through a relationship with God and the revelation of the Holy Spirit, I began to dwell on the words and seek God for answers. I am trusting He will reveal truths to me that might also be beneficial to you, and the words written here will spark your own journey to know and understand the will of God for your life.

Even though Jesus taught these lessons about 2,000 years ago, they are still ones we need to be concerned about today. Maybe you have read these parables before but didn't give them much thought. Perhaps you have dealt with the subject in a Bible study, but its meaning didn't captivate you. Maybe you are reading this for the first time. I believe God has a desire that we come to know His will through these parables and I, for one, am listening. I hope you are, too.

In an attempt to unravel the mystery of Jesus' parables and find out what we need to do in order to be ready for the Bridegroom's arrival, I would like to take you along for a ride with me. On the way I will provide colourful illustrations from my experience in learning how to ride a motorcycle, my walk of faith, and a closer look into the parables.

We'll start our ride by exploring our personal interest in the adventure. We will travel along a little further to explore what we might be able to accomplish if we commit to the ride. I hope to alleviate some of the anxiety or fear you may be experiencing about being ready for this trip by going over the details needed to prepare and how you might develop skills and strategies to ensure we arrive at our final destination.

Don't be afraid—it will be fun and worthwhile. Hop on and get ready to ride!

## CHAPTER TWO

# The Decision to Hop On

Making the decision to ride on a motorcycle was not an easy one for me. It took a great deal of faith and trust in Peter that he knew what he was doing and could keep me safe. As well, he needed to convince me that riding would be fun and beneficial.

I had no doubt that riding was beneficial for Peter, as a matter of fact, it was my idea for him to ride. It started when I noticed a promotional flyer posted on a store-front window advertising a new ride group in Princeton, British Columbia, called the "Similkameen Christian Riders." The poster stated that they were affiliated with the "Christian Motorcycle Association – CMA" and were inviting people in the community to join them for rides.

This seemed to me to be a good opportunity for my husband to join a Christian group interested in having some fun while providing an opportunity to share their faith. Don't ask me why I thought Peter would be interested in riding a motorcycle because he hadn't expressed an interest in this before. I was simply thinking of the relational aspect of the group.

Regardless, I went home and said, "Honey, why don't you go to one of those meetings and see what it's all about?" He reminded me that he didn't own a bike, to which I replied, "Couldn't you ride on the back of someone else's?" He had a great laugh at my expense before he responded, "Linda, guys don't ride on the back of other guy's bikes—it's just not done. I would need to get my own bike."

Peter did attend a couple of meetings, found he enjoyed the group, so we eventually decided to purchase a motorcycle. It was a 1983 750cc blue and white Honda Interceptor (then 18 years old). The Interceptor was an awesome bike in its time—unfortunately this one had been improperly stored in a garage for many years and it needed a lot of TLC. We got it at an affordable price and, as it happened, there was a skilled mechanic in the ride group who was able to fix it up for us.

To this point, I hadn't even considered joining my husband in this adventure. The thought of motorcycle riding was as foreign to me as the thought of climbing Mount Everest. So you can imagine my reaction the next summer when my husband asked me, "Honey, would you like to join us for a ride?"

My first thought was, "Why would I want to drive my car behind a group of bikers?"

No, I realized he was asking if I would like to ride on the back of his bike.

Would I allow fear of the unknown to hold me back? My thoughts were racing: "This sport is dangerous," "I could fall off and get hurt," and "what if I got killed?" In short, I was terrified.

Peter was prepared for my reaction. He really wanted me to experience the ride with him and was armed with calm assurances, lots of relevant information, and the promise that he wouldn't let anything bad happen to me. He convinced me it would be an experience I wouldn't want to miss. I took a leap of faith and hopped on for the ride. I found he was right! I did enjoy the ride and the time I spent with him.

The initial decision to take a ride on the back of my husband's bike opened my eyes to a whole new experience. I could have chosen to keep my feet firmly planted and watch as he rode off down the road. Instead, I entered into an opportunity for something more. This was just the start for me. I had decided to hop on, but would I be willing to see it through?

This must have been something like what Jesus was describing in Matthew 25. In "The Parable of the Ten Virgins" we are told there were ten virgins looking forward to the arrival of the Bridegroom. These women all made the decision to join the wedding party. They saw that it would be beneficial and earnestly desired to join the Bridegroom to attend the wedding banquet. They really didn't want to miss out on what was coming.

When Jesus was sharing this parable, He was speaking to a large group of people who were looking to Him as a spiritual and political leader. Many would come to understand the literal meaning behind the story and thus understood that Jesus was the Bridegroom in the story.

Isaiah referred to God as a Bridegroom who rejoices over us:

### Isaiah 62:5b

*⁵ as a bridegroom rejoices over his bride,*

*so will your God rejoice over you.*

John the Baptist referred to himself as friend of the Bridegroom (who was Jesus):

### John 3:28-30

*²⁸ You yourselves can testify that I said, "I am not the Messiah but am sent ahead of him." ²⁹ The bride belongs to the bridegroom. The friend who attends the bridegroom waits and listens for him, and is full of joy when he hears the bridegroom's voice. That joy is mine, and it is now complete. ³⁰ He must become greater; I must become less.*

Jesus even referred to Himself as a Bridegroom:

### Matthew 9:14-15

*[14] Then John's disciples came and asked him, "How is it that we and the Pharisees fast often, but your disciples do not fast?"*

*[15] Jesus answered, "How can the guests of the bridegroom mourn while he is with them? The time will come when the bridegroom will be taken from them; then they will fast."*

In the New Testament, Paul wrote to the Corinthians and described them as a virgin for Christ:

### 2 Corinthians 11:2-3

*[2] I am jealous for you with a godly jealousy. I promised you to one husband, to Christ, so that I might present you as a pure virgin to him. [3] But I am afraid that just as Eve was deceived by the serpent's cunning, your minds may somehow be led astray from your sincere and pure devotion to Christ.*

The above references confirm that Jesus' teaching in the parable refers to Himself as the Bridegroom and His chosen people, believers in Christ, as the bridesmaids who are keeping the lamps burning until the wedding banquet when they will no longer be separated.

If I want to see myself as one of the bridesmaids in the parable, I need to be qualified. I need to be identified as a Christian, set apart in a relationship with Christ through repentance of my sins, receiving forgiveness, and trusting in Jesus as my Lord and Saviour.

The following passage affirms the joy we can experience when we choose to be set apart for God:

**Proverbs 8:32-35**

*32 Now then, my children, listen to me;*

*blessed are those who keep my ways.*

*33 Listen to my instruction and be wise;*

*do not disregard it.*

*34 Blessed are those who listen to me,*

*watching daily at my doors,*

*waiting at my doorway.*

*³⁵ For those who find me find life
and receive favor from the LORD.*

Ask yourself, "Have I accepted God's offer to trust in Him with my life? Am I willing to count myself as someone set apart for God?"

If you haven't considered this as an option before, let me encourage you to read further about what a relationship with God can be like and how it will not only benefit your life, but bring you into the fullness and purpose that God has planned for you.

If your answer is yes, you have accepted Jesus as your Lord and Saviour, then let's continue to find out how we can prepare to be ready for our Bridegroom.

## CHAPTER THREE

# Why Do We Need to Get Ready?

When I was first presented with the option of riding with Peter on the back of his motorcycle, I was cautious but felt fairly confident he knew how to ride and I could trust in his abilities. I believed the rewards outweighed my fears. My main objective was to join my husband in doing something he enjoyed and therefore strengthen and build up our relationship.

I had no idea what that experience would be like. I had some recollection of swinging a leg over like getting on a horse. In some ways, I was so naive I didn't really have a concept of what could go wrong—but my husband did. He was experienced enough to know my instincts might steer me wrong. The last thing he wanted was for me to panic, choke him, and fall off the bike. The potential was real, so he lovingly took the time to explain to me what was expected by going over the ground rules for riding, such as the importance of leaning in the same direction as him rather than trying to counterbalance.

I grew in confidence because of what I was learning and soon I started thinking about taking the next step. One day I was riding on the back of Peter's bike and wondered what I would do if we had an accident and he was injured. I knew I wouldn't be able to get on the bike to ride for help. We would be selling the old Honda soon because my husband had upgraded to a newer one. If there was a good opportunity for me to learn to operate a bike, now was the time.

I have to admit that Peter was shocked that I was even interested, so before I had a chance to change my mind, I was soon entrenched in learning how to ride on my own. Being ready to ride requires more than willingness; it requires getting an education, practicing skills, and being disciplined. I am a cautious person, goal setter, check-list maker, and organizer at heart. So when it came to learning how to ride, I took it one step at a time, making sure I set a firm foundation and eliminated risk by taking precautionary measures.

Even with all that in place, I wasn't fully ready until I had the confidence, knowledge, experience, and license to ride.

As I became a more accomplished rider I found many more great reasons to ride! We often plan little overnight get-a-ways to wonderful locations. We will map out a trip based on quiet winding roads, charming scenery, and a cozy bed and breakfast to relax at after a four- or five-hour ride. My husband knows I love to enjoy the beauty and majesty of waterfalls, so we also try to incorporate some of them into the trip.

We certainly enjoy having fun together and we often meet new friends along the way. We can easily start up conversations with other motorcyclists who have similar interests. As well, we enjoy sharing our faith and shining the light of Jesus for others to see.

Similarly, Jesus had a primary objective in His ministry and life on earth—to introduce people to the person of God and invite them into a relationship with Him which would lead to the reward of an eternity spent with God in His kingdom of Heaven. Jesus' purpose was to reach all people with a message of hope and salvation. He had a mandate to reveal the identity of His Father and what He requires of us.

Jesus' objective in sharing parables was to give us a way of connecting to the stories personally and emotionally. We could identify with the characters and therefore have an understanding of the will of God and this would likely provoke a response in us. If we listen with faith and humility we can begin to understand as we are able to receive what Jesus wishes to speak to our hearts.

To start off "The Parable of the Ten Virgins," Jesus states what the kingdom of Heaven will be like. He immediately shifts our thinking from our personal experiences on earth to a heavenly perspective with the reminder that one day we will be in Heaven with Him.

Jesus then brings us to an understanding that some of the virgins will be foolish and some will be wise. Right away, we may put ourselves into the story and wonder what it would take to be wise rather than foolish. The drama unfolds as Jesus states the requirements for being ready for the Bridegroom. The parable indicates that providing light is vital to success and the light needs to be fuelled by oil readily on hand.

Next, Jesus provides a warning about the danger of not having enough oil. He states that those who aren't prepared for His return may find themselves permanently separated from Him.

God doesn't want that to happen, and is therefore giving us the heads-up. It is God's desire that everyone would be welcomed at the wedding banquet in Heaven. This is why it is important for us to come to an understanding of God's ground rules for our lives. The more I read and study the Bible with the purpose of learning from it, either on my own or with other people in Bible study groups or through sermons given in church, the more I can live my life with intention, doing what is necessary to get ready for His return.

God's ground rules were established at the time of creation and are just as relevant today. The Bible is full of references to God speaking to people in order to clearly show us the standards toward which we should strive. A great acronym for the Bible is B.I.B.L.E: Basic Instructions Before Leaving Earth.

For many years I was spiritually in the dark about God's expectations. I was unable to see the guideposts God placed before me. Instead of being able to walk confidently into my future with God, I took tentative steps, unsure and having to feel my way forward. I knew I needed God in my life but I wasn't able to make the connection. He felt distant even though I was raised as a Catholic and our family attended Mass every Sunday.

I participated in the Sacraments of Baptism, Confirmation, and Holy Communion, not fully buying into or understanding their purpose, but accepting the principles I was taught and obediently taking the steps. I remember going to regular confession but not believing or understanding I was a sinner. I would often make up sins to confess because I didn't know what to say. I was a shy, introverted child and a people pleaser—especially with my parents—and I didn't think I had done anything wrong.

Church, to me, was boring. My attitude was poor and I was also quick to be critical if I didn't enjoy the song selection or the sermon. When it came to tithing, I would give money in the same way I would pay admission to a show.

I stopped going to church after I moved out of my parents' home. I didn't follow God's standards regarding my relationships with men and lived with my first husband, Howard, before we married. He was not a Christian, had little religious upbringing, and didn't have any interest in going to church.

It wasn't until after our first child was born that I began to seek a connection with God again. I wanted to have our daughter baptized because I wanted God's protection over her and I also felt pressure from my sister who believed baptism was vital. I soon found out there were conditions to the baptism, one of which was committing to take our daughter to church regularly so she could learn about God. I started attending church again with our daughter, and my husband would sometimes attend an Easter or Christmas Mass.

Not long after our second daughter was born, we went through a series of major crises in our life. We had to close our business, claim bankruptcy, move back to our home town, and start over. This sent my husband into depression and after just six years of marriage, he ended his life. I can't begin to describe to you the utter helplessness and pain I felt.

By the age of 26, I had already experienced many losses. I was without a husband, without life insurance, without credit, and fully responsible for two children under the age of five. My faith was weak and I wondered if God even cared as I cried out to Him. When I look back, I wonder how I survived.

I packed up the girls and moved to where my Dad and his wife lived. They were a great support to me and I am thankful for their love and guidance. They were attending a Baptist church and encouraged me to attend with them, which I eventually did. I started to understand God's ground rules by watching people who were very involved in exercising their faith in the church and out in the community, and my understanding of God grew.

Then God showed me the path to a personal relationship with Him. On the first Sunday of Advent, Pastor Jack invited our family to read a passage of scripture and light the first candle. I felt honoured to be asked and humbly agreed. I read the scripture, then lit a match and held it to the candle. The flame was strong and bright.

We returned to our seats as the service continued, and before us the candle continued to glow. The time came for the children to leave for Sunday School classes and the pastor began his sermon. I will remember the impact of that sermon for the rest of my life because it was through that message I began my relationship with God.

Pastor Jack preached on this passage from the Gospel of Matthew:

**Matthew 5:14-20**

[14] *You are the light of the world. A town built on a hill cannot be hidden.* [15] *Neither do people light a lamp*

*and put it under a bowl. Instead they put it on its stand, and it gives light to everyone in the house.* [16] *In the same way, let your light shine before others, that they may see your good deeds and glorify your Father in heaven.*

[17] *Do not think that I have come to abolish the Law or the Prophets; I have not come to abolish them but to fulfill them.* [18] *For truly I tell you, until heaven and earth disappear, not the smallest letter, not the least stroke of a pen, will by any means disappear from the Law until everything is accomplished.* [19] *Therefore anyone who sets aside one of the least of these commands and teaches others accordingly will be called least in the kingdom of heaven, but whoever practices and teaches these commands will be called great in the kingdom of heaven.* [20] *For I tell you that unless your righteousness surpasses that of the Pharisees and the teachers of the law, you will certainly not enter the kingdom of heaven.*

Jesus made it clear in this passage that as believers we represent God to others through our conduct and character measured by the fulfillment of the Law. I began to dwell on the Ten Commandments which I had learned as a child. I saw myself as a "good person," an example to others, and thought I behaved in a way that pleased God.

Then the Holy Spirit began to work in my heart. I realized my nature and character were a gift from God—not something I had earned. I also realized God could use me the way I was for His kingdom's purposes if I made myself a willing vessel for Him.

God reminded me that to this point in my life I had been seeking Him to serve me. My prayers were for His action in my life. I was in a one-way relationship with Him where I was completely selfish, thinking only in terms of what God could do for me rather than what I could do for God.

God then focused my attention down the page of the Bible from Matthew 5:21 through to chapter 6, where greater meaning regarding the commandments was highlighted:

### Matthew 6:22-23

[22] *The eye is the lamp of the body. If your eyes are healthy, your whole body will be full of light.* [23] *But if your eyes are unhealthy, your whole body will be full*

*of darkness. If then the light within you is darkness, how great is that darkness!*

I was becoming more and more convicted of my shortcomings and the sin of which I remained unrepentant. The Holy Spirit nudged me further as Pastor Jack preached on the greatest commandment of all:

**Matthew 22:37-40**

*[37] Jesus replied: "'Love the Lord your God with all your heart and with all your soul and with all your mind.' [38] This is the first and greatest commandment. [39] And the second is like it: 'Love your neighbor as yourself.' [40] All the Law and the Prophets hang on these two commandments."*

All my life God knew me and was drawing me to Himself but I remained in the dark because of my sin of selfishness. I put myself before God and others. I trusted in my own abilities, my own nature and character, and believed I was a good person right with God. Yet that is not what the Bible teaches:

**Mark 10:18**

[18] *"Why do you call me good?" Jesus answered. "No one is good—except God alone."*

The conviction of the Holy Spirit brought me to tears. In the service that day, the people faded away and all I could focus on was the brightness of the light from the flame of the candle. God was calling me to be a light for Him, but before that could happen, I knew I needed to repent of my sin.

The service was wrapping up and Pastor Jack issued an invitation to the congregation. Anyone wishing to make a commitment to God, to be willing to let the light of God shine in their lives, was invited to come to the front of the sanctuary where someone would pray with them.

God had my attention: He had my new heart and I willingly stood that day and walked to the front. I prayed with the pastor, repented of my sin, and requested the forgiveness of God. I was ready to begin a wonderful new and living relationship with Him. I had finally found my way out of the darkness and into the light.

At the same time, God brought a new man into my life who would soon be my husband. Peter and I both became

Christians in the same church during the same period of time. We both attended the same evening Bible study group that year and were even baptised the same day in June when the lake warmed up. When we started dating, we chose to try to honour God in our relationship to the best of our ability.

These experiences gave me a new perspective on God's ground rules and through the sharing of my experience I pray you will gain a greater understanding, as well.

I have created a summary list of five important guiding principles God gave us so that we could have a deeper relationship with Him and live a victorious life. I encourage you to pray for God to reveal even more to you. Do your own research and add to the list as the Lord directs.

1. *First and foremost I believe we are to love God with all our heart, soul, mind, and strength. Do you love God in this way? Are you able to express your love for God through your daily life?*

2. *We are to love our neighbours as ourselves. We are selfish by nature. We understand what we expect from others in terms of love. Do you think you are*

*able to love others with the love God expects from you?*

3. *We are to follow the commandments God provided to Moses as recorded in Exodus 20, Deuteronomy 5 and 6, and in Matthew 5. Have you considered these commandments and do you strive to live up to the standards God has laid out for us?*

4. *We are to be good stewards of all the resources God has given us. There are over 2,000 references in the Bible that relate to this subject alone. If you have money, do you share it generously? Do you use your gifts and abilities to help and encourage others?*

5. *We are to be ambassadors for God by sharing what we know with others. This is our "Great Commission." Some references to this subject are: Matthew 28, Mark 16, Acts 8, 1 Corinthians 1, and 1 Thessalonians. Do you share your faith with others? Are people drawn toward your light, asking what it is that you have, and wanting some of it?*

I believe these disciplines are just some of the ways we maintain our relationship with God.

As I shared in my personal story, I believe Jesus was implying we are the lamps and the light of God shines through us as we live our lives bringing glory to Him. When Jesus returns for you, will He see the light in you, or have you fallen asleep in your faith without having enough oil left in reserve?

The following verses highlight our responsibility:

**1 Peter 2:9-11**

*⁹ But you are a chosen people, a royal priesthood, a holy nation, God's special possession, that you may declare the praises of him who called you out of darkness into his wonderful light. ¹⁰ Once you were not a people, but now you are the people of God; once you had not received mercy, but now you have received mercy.*
*¹¹ Dear friends, I urge you, as foreigners and exiles, to abstain from sinful desires, which wage war against your soul.*

The ground rules Jesus is trying to convey through "The Parable of the Ten Virgins" are of great importance. His message is a reminder of what God expects from us. This is a good time to re-evaluate the understanding you have regarding your purpose and responsibility toward God.

Has your understanding become fuzzy? Have you let life get in the way of meeting God's expectations? Is your light shining for Christ?

Let's examine this further in the next chapter as we develop a road map for success.

# CHAPTER FOUR

# The Road Map for Success

We have spent time together in the initial chapters looking at some of the basic elements of being ready. We recognized the importance of making the decision to hop on and then examined why we need to get ready. In relation to "The Parable of the Ten Virgins," we have come to understand these elements, as follows:

1. We have received an important warning—Jesus will return at any time and we need to be ready. This means that life as we know it today will end, and if we are ready, a celebration of new life in a new Heaven on earth will begin. As the parable described, the Bridegroom (who is Jesus) will come for us and

we are to be prepared by having enough oil (spiritual fuel) to be ready for His arrival (return) in order to go to the wedding banquet (celebration of His return). If we are not ready, we will miss our chance to attend the banquet (enter into the new kingdom), and we will forever be outside (in death).

2. We first needed to decide whether we were going to participate. In the context of the parable, all 10 virgins had a desire to attend the wedding banquet with the Bridegroom when He arrived. If you have chosen not to participate in the past, it is my prayer that you have now had a change of heart!

3. We came to an understanding of the importance of being wise rather than being foolish. We need to learn God's ground rules and what preparations might be required in order to be ready. The bridesmaids all had a desire to meet with the Bridegroom, but some were obviously sitting back, unconcerned about what might happen if they had a long wait. Jesus is warning us that we shouldn't be complacent while we are waiting.

4. We also came to understand that the oil (spiritual fuel) which the 10 virgins had in their lamps was gen-

erated through their love for the Bridegroom (Jesus) and by doing what honours and pleases Him.

Now comes the time to develop a road map that will help to sustain us. We are at various stages of developing our love and faith in God, and may not always be on the right road. In other words, we can all do better. The following information is meant to encourage you to stay the course by developing strategies for success.

**Avoiding Delays, Distractions, and Roadblocks**

In the past few years I have experienced some delays, distractions, and roadblocks that have kept me from riding as often as I would like. For example, I delay riding when the weather is cold or rainy because I would rather stay warm and dry. There are times I can't ride because my bike needs some maintenance or repairs. I have been distracted by a lack of planning or a busy schedule. Sometimes there are roadblocks or last-minute cancellations because of unexpected visitors. As well, I had some minor spills which could have derailed me, had I given up and quit. I have met several people who have told me they used to ride but decided to quit and sell their bikes because of similar issues.

I think the same can happen in our Christian walk. I have heard people say they still considered themselves Christians but things got complicated and they drifted away from church and doing the things they knew would honour God. The following are some reasons for complacency I have heard:

*"I don't have enough time in the day to read my Bible or pray and when I do find time I fall asleep right away."*

*"My husband is not a believer and wants me to spend time with him instead of going to church, so I find it easier to stay at home rather than argue with him."*

*"I work full-time and don't have any extra time to devote to ministry. Besides, I don't have any ministry training or abilities to offer."*

*"I thought that people who go to church would be trustworthy, but I was proven wrong. Frankly, I would rather not go to church than to see them again."*

*"I was offended when the pastor preached about some of my sins. He doesn't understand my reasons and I don't think he is in a position to judge me."*

*"The Christian faith doesn't interest me anymore."*

God's ground rules are not easy and many have given up trying to obey them. The work may seem too difficult and the time investment too great. It is heartbreaking to me when I see fellow Christians drifting away from God's plans and purposes. I want to cry out, "Wake up! Where is your passion for God? Why are you giving up?"

They say they still believe in God and expect they will meet up with me in Heaven. I sure hope that is true. However, when I read "The Parable of the Ten Virgins," I wonder why it is all ten of the virgins wanted to go to the wedding banquet with the Bridegroom, however, five went off looking for extra oil and were too late when the Bridegroom arrived.

I worry there are many Christians who are being delayed, or are letting too many distractions get in their way. Maybe there are some major roadblocks to overcome. There are many possible reasons, however, we need to be determined to overcome them. We need to have the tenacity to fight our way through the roadblocks. We need to ensure we aren't derailed because of weak or lame excuses. We need to have a plan to ensure nothing gets in our way and we are prepared when the Bridegroom comes.

**Learning the Basics**

You may have seen some funny home videos where someone hops onto a little dirt bike or motorcycle and revs the engine, takes off like a shot, and then is unable to steer or brake and ends up taking out a fence or getting caught up in some trees. Although this makes great material for a laugh, I had no interest in being the star of the show. I knew I needed to gain knowledge and understanding about motorcycles first, and then practice what I learned.

Peter volunteered to be my instructor as he had some knowledge and experience in riding. As I mentioned earlier, we chose to use the bike he first purchased when he became involved with the CMA. The bike was a 1983 Honda Interceptor. It weighed about 550 pounds and had 750cc of power. It had a droopy mirror, an idle that was either too high or too low, and signal lights that worked occasionally. Even though I thought the bike was too big and powerful for me, it was still a good choice to learn on because we hadn't invested much money in it and I didn't worry about it getting damaged.

In order for me to ride the motorcycle, I would need to obtain a Class 6 learner's license. We picked up a manual from the local insurance agency. I studied it, memorizing all the details, so I could pass the written exam.

We then reviewed the operation of the bike itself. Peter walked me around the bike while he explained the purpose of each part and how the parts worked as a whole.

Learning how motorcycles work is as foundational to successful riding as learning about God and developing a relationship with Him are foundational to exercising our faith.

When people become new believers, they may try to figure things out for themselves or seek a friend or mentor for help. They will often start attending a local church and ask the pastor for advice regarding how to gain knowledge and understanding about spiritual matters. Whether they figure things out on their own or find great training programs, one of the most important foundational strategies for success is spending time learning about God and His will and purpose for their lives.

Reading the Bible is like opening up a motorcycle manual. Everything we need to know about who God is and what He is like is available there. We have many versions of Bibles available to us and some are available with concordances or study notes or are printed in chronological order. It is good to establish a reading plan of 15 minutes to an hour each day. As we read, the Holy Spirit reveals truths about God to us so we can gain greater understanding and deepen our relationship. There are also excellent books written by Christian authors that help to broaden our knowledge on any subject as it relates to God.

Going to church and hearing the message brought by the pastor is another great way to learn. The sermons are often God-inspired and full of instruction. As well, regular Bible study time, prayer group, Sunday School programs, men's retreats, women's retreats, and family camps are all offered in order to provide sound teaching.

Jesus modeled this strategy of learning in His own life. The Bible says that as a young boy He studied from scholars and teachers, as written in the following account:

*Luke 2:41-52*

**The Boy Jesus at the Temple**

*[41] Every year Jesus' parents went to Jerusalem for the Festival of the Passover. [42] When he was twelve years old, they went up to the festival, according to the custom. [43] After the festival was over, while his parents were returning home, the boy Jesus stayed behind in Jerusalem, but they were unaware of it. [44] Thinking he was in their company, they traveled on for a day. Then they began looking for him among their relatives and friends. [45] When they did not find him, they went back to Jerusalem to look for him. [46] After three days they found him in the temple courts, sitting among the teachers, listening to them and asking them questions. [47] Everyone who heard him was amazed at his understanding and his answers. [48] When his parents saw him, they were astonished. His mother said to him, "Son, why have you treated*

*us like this? Your father and I have been anxiously searching for you."*

*⁴⁹ "Why were you searching for me?" he asked. "Didn't you know I had to be in my Father's house?" ⁵⁰ But they did not understand what he was saying to them.*

*⁵¹ Then he went down to Nazareth with them and was obedient to them. But his mother treasured all these things in her heart. ⁵² And Jesus grew in wisdom and stature, and in favor with God and man.*

The best teacher is God Himself. We can develop our relationship with Him by spending time getting to know Him, communicating with Him, putting our trust in Him, and doing things that honour and please Him.

**Spending Time Communicating**

God will speak to us in many ways and we need to learn how to be tuned in to Him when He speaks. In the book of James, the writer exhorts Christians to listen:

### James 1:19

*[19] My dear brothers and sisters, take note of this: Everyone should be quick to listen, slow to speak and slow to become angry ....*

One of the ways to please our Heavenly Father is to sit at His feet listening to every word He says with great interest, with a desire to learn and to be in awe of Him. In the story of Mary and Martha caring for the needs of Jesus, we learn that Jesus is pleased when we are still and focusing on Him:

### Luke 10:38-42

*[38] As Jesus and his disciples were on their way, he came to a village where a woman named Martha opened her home to him. [39] She had a sister called Mary, who sat at the Lord's feet listening to what he said. [40] But Martha was distracted by all the preparations that had to be made. She came to him and asked, "Lord, don't you care that my sister has left me to do the work by myself? Tell her to help me!"*

*[41] "Martha, Martha," the Lord answered, "you are worried and upset about many things, [42] but few things are needed—or indeed only one. Mary has*

*chosen what is better, and it will not be taken away
from her."*

If Jesus came to visit me, I would want to spend all of my
time with Him, learning about His interests, His family, and
His history. What made Him the person He is today? Why
did He make the decisions He made? What does He appreciate in others? Where did He feel it was most important to
put His time, and even what made Him laugh? I would want
to know everything possible.

***God communicates through the Bible.*** When we are
seeking a message from God regarding an aspect of our
lives, we can be sure He will speak to us through the Bible,
which is God-inspired. I once received tremendous comfort
from God when His word reassured me I could trust in Him.

When my youngest daughter was 10 years old, she
and I joined several families from our church for a summer
adventure. We went camping overnight and then planned
to spend a lovely summer afternoon drifting on inflatable
rafts down a calm section of the Kettle River into the community of Rock Creek. That day things didn't go as planned
and my daughter nearly drowned as a result. I was unable

to do anything to save her but another person in our group came to her rescue.

That night, my mind wouldn't rest; the horrible scene replayed over and over and I was not able to fall asleep. I felt totally helpless in the situation and full of guilt that I wasn't able to do something to save my daughter who called out to me again and again. When I could stand it no longer, I climbed out of bed and found my Bible. I prayed that God would speak to me and give me relief from this trauma. I randomly opened the Bible and started to read from the book of Titus. As I read, my spirit was drawn to the following passage:

**Titus 3:4-5**
*[4] But when the kindness and love of God our Savior appeared, [5] he saved us, not because of righteous things we had done, but because of his mercy. He saved us through the washing of rebirth and renewal by the Holy Spirit ....*

I realized God was offering me the comfort of knowing He had saved my daughter. She was saved because of HIS MERCY. I didn't have to be in control, I only needed to trust

Him. I was able to start praising God and thanking Him for giving my daughter additional years. I also thanked Him for the peace He had given me as I drifted off into a deep sleep, knowing He was in control.

**God speaks to you in your prayers.** Without a doubt, God will speak to you as you pray. You may suddenly feel peace in a stressful situation over which you have no control. You may receive confirmation in your prayer or sense a direction God wants you to take. It is a good idea to journal your prayers so you can look back and see how God answered your prayers.

**God speaks through worship songs.** I often find the songs chosen for a Sunday worship time will speak to me directly. They will comfort me, or exhort me. They will help direct my thoughts and my mind back to Jesus. Many people have found God will write a song in their heart and they will write out the words and the songs will speak to others.

**God speaks through sermons.** Pastors or ministers receive messages from God for His people. You can certainly expect to hear from God during a sermon. He will convict you of sin or exhort you to love and good works. He will speak to you through your own experiences. God spoke to me most clearly at the time of my salvation.

***God communicates through others.*** Christians who have developed good listening skills toward God will often be given words to share with others. I really appreciate when I am a recipient of a message from God through others; my ears are immediately tuned to hear from Him.

***God speaks to us through our dreams.*** In recent years, thousands of Muslims have come to salvation through a personal relationship with Jesus Christ as a result of dreams, visions, and angelic visits. Often there can be messages for us in our dreams. I find it a good practice to write out my dream when I wake up. I have often received inspiration or direction for this book through my dreams. We do, however, need to be discerning.

***God's spiritual promptings.*** I call these "nigglers." Often people have a sense they should do something right away but will ignore it. For example, I was once prompted to phone a cousin whose mother had recently passed away. At first I resisted the urging because I felt awkward and uncomfortable reaching out to her. I listened to the prompt, however, and was blessed by a delightful hour-long conversation during which I shared my love for God and brought her to a place of understanding and peace. Promptings of the Holy

Spirit might be there for us to take action, to help others, to take care of something we forgot, and even to keep us safe.

***Hearing God through presentations and other resources.*** I have often felt moved by the Spirit to donate to groups or organizations following presentations or when I have read testimonials or even seen a small ad in a magazine. I know in my spirit when God wants me to donate and I have been blessed in doing so. When God urges me to share my resources, I feel it's important to listen and obey. God's way of helping other people in need is through people like you and me. I have heard many stories about how God has moved people to help others and thereby become the answer to their prayers.

***Hearing God through a Bible study.*** Years ago I was part of a women's Bible study in which God was teaching us to seek the truth rather than believe in gossip. We had a lively discussion about recent events followed by a time of prayer. The hot topic was a newspaper article that stated a mother of two teen girls was being charged for selling drugs to students. Several of us were quick to judge her but God was reminding us to seek the truth first.

I felt convicted by my response to the article and suggested someone visit the woman and find out her story.

Others suggested we put together a care package of groceries in order to show her God loved her and He desired to bring out the truth. I was quickly nominated to take the package and talk with her since I felt so strongly about God's word on this matter.

A few days later, I showed up at her door, presented the gift, and stated my case. She immediately broke down and wept and invited me in so she could share her side of the story. She proceeded to tell me the night before she considered taking her life and she cried out to God to help her because she couldn't deal with the lies, the possibility of losing her children, and going to jail. She said that through my visit God had answered her prayer.

**Developing Trust**

Trust was an important aspect of learning how to ride a motorcycle. Trust in the bike, trust in myself, trust in my instructor, and trust in the environment around me. Without trust, I would not have the confidence to get on the bike and ride.

I believe trust in God is also a vital aspect of our relationship. I remember when I was under a great deal of stress because my oldest daughter, who was about 15 years old at the time, was being a real "pill" and had run away from home. In other words, the choices she was making were putting her in a lot of danger and it was hard for me to see her making such bad decisions (hard to "swallow"). I came to the point that I had to pray, "Lord, I entrust my daughter to You. Please do whatever it takes to save her." I trusted God to do whatever He thought was best. If you, as a parent, have ever had to pray that prayer, you know how difficult it is to surrender complete control and trust that God will intervene for you even if you may not like the way He does it.

At that time I felt I needed to get into my car and go look for her. And, as God fulfilled my prayer, I found her on the highway hitchhiking. I picked her up and we talked about what was going on in her life over the past few days. I asked her to consider moving to her Auntie's for a while. She agreed, we picked up her things, and she got on a Greyhound bus within the hour. God intervened in her life in a profound way and spared her from an uncertain future.

Do you trust God with your life? How about with the lives of your spouse and children? God is trustworthy. Spend time looking at the promises He makes to us in His word.

**Putting on Protective Gear**

We have to do more than just trust in God. We also need to do our part in ensuring our safety by putting on protective gear.

When riding a motorcycle, it is important to wear protective armour so that, God forbid, if there is an accident or a spill, the gear will protect you from injury and even death. I started off with a pair of work gloves; an imitation leather bomber jacket from the sale rack at the local thrift store; a pair of old boots from the dump that we spray-painted black; and a borrowed helmet that was three sizes too large (imagine trying to do a shoulder check when the helmet doesn't move with your head).

Then over the next few years, we purchased armoured gloves, pants, boots, and a jacket. Finally, we bought a snug, certified helmet to protect my head. It may seem as though we were being over protective, however, I knew I had done everything possible to ensure my safety should I be thrown from the bike.

The Bible has instructions about putting on protective gear as referenced in Ephesians 6:10-18. I like to dress in my spiritual armour every morning before I head off to work. I'll pray the word of God in my own words:

*Good morning, Lord. Thank You for this day You have given me. Help me to be strong and courageous in Your mighty power. I love You, Lord, and I thank You for all You are going to do in my life today.*

*I now buckle the Belt of Truth around my waist which maintains my integrity. I put on the Breastplate of Righteousness which protects my emotions and silences accusations. My feet are fitted with the readiness that comes from the gospel of peace.*

*I take up the Shield of Faith that is my defence, providing me with trust in You and protection from fear, doubt, and confusion that come at me like flaming arrows from the enemy. I place the Helmet of Salvation over my head which protects me from becoming deceived, doubtful, and discouraged.*

*I take up the Sword of the Spirit which is my only offensive weapon. It is Your Holy Word, the Bible, the authority over all the power of the enemy. I will speak its truths in the face of my enemies.*

*And I will pray in the Spirit at all times so that You will provide me with wisdom and discernment to do Your will and You will fill each of my needs as they arise.*

Jesus understood the importance of putting on spiritual protection before entering a battle. The Bible gives an account about Jesus first going down to the River Jordan, being baptized, and receiving the Holy Spirit (Luke 3:21-22). He was then led into the desert and challenged by Satan to exchange His relationship with God for worldly power and wealth. Jesus had the protection of the knowledge of who He was in relationship with God and when He was challenged, He used the Word of God to come out the victor. Hear what He says when tempted in the wilderness:

### Luke 4:1-13
[1] *Jesus, full of the Holy Spirit, left the Jordan and was led by the Spirit into the wilderness, [2] where for forty days he was tempted by the devil. He ate nothing*

during those days, and at the end of them he was hungry.

[3] The devil said to him, "If you are the Son of God, tell this stone to become bread."

[4] Jesus answered, "It is written: 'Man shall not live on bread alone.'"

[5] The devil led him up to a high place and showed him in an instant all the kingdoms of the world. [6] And he said to him, "I will give you all their authority and splendor; it has been given to me, and I can give it to anyone I want to. [7] If you worship me, it will all be yours."

[8] Jesus answered, "It is written: 'Worship the Lord your God and serve him only.'"

[9] The devil led him to Jerusalem and had him stand on the highest point of the temple. "If you are the Son of God," he said, "throw yourself down from here. [10] For it is written:

"'He will command his angels concerning you
to guard you carefully;

[11] they will lift you up in their hands,
so that you will not strike your foot against a stone.'"

*¹² Jesus answered, "It is said: 'Do not put the Lord your God to the test.'"*
*¹³ When the devil had finished all this tempting, he left him until an opportune time.*

Jesus learned to persevere and not give up because He was fully clothed in protective armour and was able to withstand the fiery darts sent by Satan.

**Putting what You Know into Practice**

After learning all about the motorcycle I would be riding, and passing the Motor Vehicle written exam, and being outfitted in protective armour, I was then able to start practicing riding. During the practice sessions I dropped the bike on myself on a couple of occasions, but I didn't sustain any injuries. A few times I thought I wasn't cut out for this adventure and felt like quitting, but continued to persevere.

After many practice sessions and gaining more confidence in my riding ability, I went through the Skills Test routine that was the next stage in the licensing process. Once I was able to ride smoothly at a slow speed, get around obstacles, make a sharp turn, completely change directions in a small space, and brake quickly to avoid a crash, I was ready for the test.

Peter and I arrived at the exam site and waited for my turn. As I watched the person before me, my anxiety grew. I began riding slowly through the course obstacles and made a few nice turns. Next I was asked to make a tight left U-turn. Halfway around the bend I felt unstable and dropped my foot to keep my balance. Boom—instant failure! Touching the ground with a foot during the Skills Test is not permitted. My confidence slipped a little—but I did not quit.

My husband and I continued to ride and practice together over the following few weeks while waiting for the next available exam time slot. It would be in about a month's time. We took time off work, again, for me to take the test, and—you may have guessed it—I failed. I believed the bike was too big for me and I developed even greater test anxiety.

I persevered until I passed the Skills Test at the end of the riding season. We held a celebration, then promptly parked the bike for the winter. I felt great having finally accomplished that goal. I had one more test to do to achieve my full Class 6 license.

The following year, when the weather warmed up and the rainy season was done, I continued to practice riding in order to prepare for the Road Test. Once I felt comfortable riding again, I booked an appointment for the test. Unfortunately, I failed the exam for failing to slow down in a playground zone. I was undaunted, because I thought it may have been premature to expect myself to feel comfortable after not riding for eight months.

I went into the licensing office to rebook the test, only to find out my learner's license had expired and I was now required to begin the entire testing process over again—#!@?>. I was not a happy camper. By this time, Tom, the local examiner for each of my tests, was not my favourite person. I think he may have cringed when he saw me coming and I did the same when I saw him!

After one or two more Skills Test failures, Peter and I finally got smart and borrowed a smaller bike to use for the Skills Test. I passed easily. The time came for me to take the Road Test and things went smoothly until about three-quarters of the way through.

The temperature was very high that day and my bike engine started overheating from having to go so slowly through traffic and playground zones, and waiting for traffic signals to change. The ride was taking such a long time that I started overheating as well (I'm sure it had nothing to do with my test anxiety).

By radio, the examiner asked me to park the bike, turn it off, get off, and then point out hazards in the area. I pulled the bike into the appropriate parking position and unknowingly I accidently hit the kill switch with my right hand while reaching to turn off the key. Tom spent time with me discussing the surrounding hazards and then asked me to get back on the bike, start it, and ride back to the licensing office.

I got back on the bike but was unable to start it. I was sure it was because the bike had overheated. Tom accepted my reasoning and agreed to come back after the bike cooled to complete the test. While I was waiting, I peeled off my jacket, took a deep breath, then it dawned on me to check the kill switch. Sure enough, I had it in the OFF position.

When Tom came back I was ready to ride. I passed the exam and we made peace with each other. To this day I wonder if he knew about the kill switch but chose to let me figure it out for myself.

What a great accomplishment for me! I was finally awarded a Class 6 license after two riding seasons. I worked hard and it paid off. I didn't give up and I learned many lessons in the process. In hindsight, however, even though we were sure we had a good strategy, it wasn't the best.

I now recommend to women interested in learning how to ride to enrol in a motorcycle training program. It is the best investment of time and money and a great way to build a solid foundation and avoid developing bad habits.

When we first become Christians, we understand we are new creations and therefore we need to start practicing to walk in our new-found faith. We can either try to figure out for ourselves what we need to practice, or we can learn what is required through a Basic Christianity or Discipleship Training program.

Some of the disciplines you might practice are:

- Join a local church
- Use your gifts and abilities for the benefit of others
- Pray for the needs of others, considering health, social issues, and salvation
- Teach Sunday School
- Become a mentor to new or immature Christians
- Be generous with your resources
- Encourage others
- Be involved in church leadership
- Show grace and kindness to others

The following verses in the Bible spell this out:

**Romans 12:6-8**

*[6] We have different gifts, according to the grace given to each of us. If your gift is prophesying, then prophesy in accordance with your faith; [7] if it is serving, then serve; if it is teaching, then teach; [8] if it is to encourage, then give encouragement; if it is giving, then give generously; if it is to lead, do it diligently; if it is to show mercy, do it cheerfully.*

As well, if we look at the ministry of Jesus, we can find other examples of Christian disciplines to practice. Start reading through the Gospel accounts of Jesus' ministry. They all give testimony of Jesus' teaching, preaching, gathering disciples, sharing resources, driving out demons, healing people, and more.

As Christians, we will be tempted, by Satan, to give up our Christian faith and go back to living a worldly life. The lure of sinful practices is ever present. We need to remain steadfast in our faith as Jesus did, and God promises us help.

## Regular Maintenance

Every time Peter and I take a trip with our motorcycles, I feel fantastic. I think back to the struggles and challenges I endured as a rider-in-training in order to get to where I am today, and I am so thankful I persevered. Riding is not without its challenges, but I have built self-assurance to the point that I can throw my leg over the bike and ride without any of the earlier anxiety.

Even with this confidence, however, I am reminded that I need to do regular maintenance on the bike to ensure it operates safely. Before each road trip, it is my responsibility to walk around the bike with a wet rag and clean it, affording me the opportunity to look it over. I check the oil, the fuel situation, the air in the tires, and look for any loose parts, as well. If I neglect this responsibility I could end up on the side of the road with problems.

The same goes for our spiritual lives. If we don't take the responsibility of doing a self check-up, we may find we are deflated or our oil is low when it comes to our relationship with Christ. Sometimes it is good to have someone else do a check for us and hopefully point out areas in our lives that are suffering neglect.

# CHAPTER FIVE

# Roadside Assistance

When I prepare to head out on my motorcycle, I try to ensure nothing gets in the way of my goal to ride. Hopefully I am well rested and am looking forward to the trip. I put on my protective gear to keep me safe. I unwrap my bike and walk around it to confirm everything is in good working order. I check the oil and the fuel gauge to ensure I have enough supply for the trip.

I trust I have done everything I can to be ready. I know how the bike works and what I need to do to operate it. I have put my knowledge into practice. I have developed my skills. While I still make mistakes, I try to keep my focus. But with all of these things in place, I know there is still an element of risk.

Whenever I ride, I take certain risks, particularly if I am tired, anxious, or afraid. I have to ride defensively and be alert for hazards, wildlife, and other vehicles in my path. It might turn out the trip is farther than I expected and I run low on fuel.

As I was writing this book, my husband approached me with a new gadget for the bikes. It was a siphon hose. He explained to me that if one of us runs out of fuel we could siphon fuel from one bike to the other to get us to the next fuel stop. This made sense to me because my bike has a larger fuel tank than his.

I asked him, "What if that left both of us short? Wouldn't we both be sitting on the side of the road unable to continue the journey?" He agreed this could happen but the hose could be helpful if one bike was able to make it to the next fuel stop, fill up, then return and transfer fuel to the other bike. This would mean one of us would need to wait while the other went for fuel.

Another option, he suggested, would be to purchase fuel from a passing motorist so we wouldn't use up either of our supplies. His suggestions seemed reasonable and I felt secure in having a plan or strategy that should work to ensure we got to our destination. I was fairly confident that a passing motorist would be willing to help us out.

When I considered the implications of sharing fuel with my husband, it occurred to me that the same concept could relate to "The Parable of the Ten Virgins." Originally, it seemed odd to me that the five wise bridesmaids refused to share their oil with the five foolish ones. However, it made sense once I realized it could cause all of them to run short. It was far better for each of them to carry their own additional fuel.

In the previous chapters we learned that by loving God and getting to know His will for our lives, and then putting into practice what He asks of us, we have a better chance of being prepared for His return. This is the main source of our fuel—knowing and loving God and being obedient to Him. However, we need to be aware that even though there are things we ought to be doing to sustain our relationship with God, what we do is not going to be enough. We need to have access to an additional source of fuel.

As the parable indicates, we may run too low and may not be able to replenish it in time. At the last minute, desire was not enough to make extra oil appear. No, the extra oil needed to be purchased in advance of the Bridegroom's arrival, but instead, the virgins were trying to obtain it when the Bridegroom arrived.

I think many people, Christian or non-Christian, believe that at the last minute before Jesus comes, they will be given the opportunity to say a quick prayer of repentance and ask for help, then expect by His grace He will still let them into Heaven.

Some people might think they are basically good people, and by trying to live a good life, Jesus will overlook their transgressions and welcome them in, no questions asked.

Others think they can earn their way into Heaven without even knowing Jesus. They believe if they work hard enough doing what will please Him, He will recognize their service and invite them in.

That is not what Jesus intended to portray through "The Parable of the Ten Virgins." The parable stated that the five virgins who were ready for the Bridegroom had actually prepared by obtaining extra oil. This is the crucial point to the story and one we really need to pay attention to if we are going to be fully prepared for the Lord's return.

I believe we need to explore what Jesus is trying to say to us if we expect good results. I would like to suggest to you that the extra oil (spiritual fuel) comes from, or is developed by, what we do within the context of being in relationship with Him.

In fact, our fuel can only be refilled by an outside source—the Holy Spirit. The extra fuel I needed was actually provided when I repented of my sin and asked the Lord Jesus to take control of my life. At that time, I was given the Holy Spirit as my helper.

I can choose to accept the Holy Spirit and allow Him to reign in me, relinquishing control over my life and allowing His leading instead. Then I don't have to depend on my own abilities. When Jesus rose to Heaven He said He would provide a Counsellor for us. He said we would be far better off than if He was by our side because we could access help directly from the Holy Spirit. This is indicated in John 16:

### John 16:7

*⁷ But very truly I tell you, it is for your good that I am going away. Unless I go away, the Advocate will not come to you; but if I go, I will send him to you.*

The Holy Spirit is God in us. He is the extra fuel that is accessible to each of us. However, we need to ask for Him and allow Him in. Just like a siphon hose, if both ends are not connected, the fuel cannot be transferred. If you run out of fuel and Jesus arrives before you are ready, you may be out of luck. We need the Holy Spirit for a reason, because without Him, we will never be prepared for the Lord's return.

When I repented of my sin and asked the Lord Jesus to take control of my life, I received the Holy Spirit as my helper, but I have to be careful not to disconnect from Him and start trusting more in myself. He is the greatest gift we receive from Jesus and He became accessible to us through Christ's death and resurrection.

Now God says, in His Holy Word, that we need to remain in Him and He in us. This connection is vital to having a purposeful and successful life. He states we will provide good fruit as indicated in John 15:

### John 15:1-4

[1] *"I am the true vine, and my Father is the gardener.*
[2] *He cuts off every branch in me that bears no fruit, while every branch that does bear fruit he prunes so that it will be even more fruitful.* [3] *You are already clean because of the word I have spoken to you.* [4] *Remain in me, as I also remain in you. No branch*

*can bear fruit by itself; it must remain in the vine. Neither can you bear fruit unless you remain in me.*

As we look at the bridesmaids in "The Parable of the Ten Virgins," we notice they cannot help each other by sharing their own oil. Extra oil needed to be purchased through an outside source. Our spiritual fuel is generated through the Holy Spirit. This is further described in the following passages.

By faith we receive righteousness through the Holy Spirit:

### Galatians 5:4-6

*[4] You who are trying to be justified by the law have been alienated from Christ; you have fallen away from grace. [5] For through the Spirit we eagerly await by faith the righteousness for which we hope. [6] For in Christ Jesus neither circumcision nor uncircumcision has any value. The only thing that counts is faith expressing itself through love.*

We receive fruit and a new nature from the Holy Spirit:

### Galatians 5:22-25

*[22] But the fruit of the Spirit is love, joy, peace, forbearance, kindness, goodness, faithfulness, [23] gentleness and self-control. Against such things there is no law. [24] Those who belong to Christ Jesus have crucified the flesh with its passions and desires. [25] Since we live by the Spirit, let us keep in step with the Spirit.*

We receive gifts of wisdom, knowledge, faith, healing, prophecy, discernment, new language, and interpretation from the Holy Spirit as He determines:

### 1 Corinthians 12:7-11

*[7] Now to each one the manifestation of the Spirit is given for the common good. [8] To one there is given through the Spirit a message of wisdom, to another a message of knowledge by means of the same Spirit, [9] to another faith by the same Spirit, to another gifts of healing by that one Spirit, [10] to another miraculous powers, to another prophecy, to another distinguishing between spirits, to another speaking in*

*different kinds of tongues, and to still another the interpretation of tongues. ¹¹ All these are the work of one and the same Spirit, and he distributes them to each one, just as he determines.*

We receive God's love that pours out of us through the Holy Spirit:

**1 Corinthians 13:1-3, 13**
*¹ If I speak in the tongues of men or of angels, but do not have love, I am only a resounding gong or a clanging cymbal. ² If I have the gift of prophecy and can fathom all mysteries and all knowledge, and if I have a faith that can move mountains, but do not have love, I am nothing. ³ If I give all I possess to the poor and give over my body to hardship that I may boast, but do not have love, I gain nothing.*
*¹³ And now these three remain: faith, hope and love. But the greatest of these is love.*

We each have a personal responsibility to ensure we do what it takes to be ready. In the end, we can't rely on others to get us through the doors. However, while we still have time, I believe God wants us to be prudent in our own preparations as well as to encourage one another toward the same goal.

Through the gifts and talents God has given us we help and encourage others. This pleases God, blesses us, and fills us with joy that shines from us and lights the way to Jesus. We do these things for the current blessings they provide, as well as for the eternal reward we will receive in Heaven. The more we invest of ourselves, the more fuel God generates in us.

So I ask you, "Are you plugged into the Holy Spirit? Are you willing to do what it takes to bear fruit? If someone were to look at your life, would they see the evidence of the Holy Spirit?"

If not, God wants you to know that time is running short. Now that you know what God expects from you, there should be no excuses when Jesus arrives. You really don't want to miss out on the celebration!

## CHAPTER SIX

# The Thrill of a Great Ride

I t is very rewarding to succeed in accomplishing our goals. The more we invest, the more we feel the sweet joy that puts a big smile on our face and a bounce in our step.

I have personally experienced this feeling of accomplishment in motorcycling. I started off thinking I could learn to ride a bike on my own. I could picture myself on an open road, bending gracefully with each curve and smoothly travelling in sync behind my husband's bike, taking in the beautiful scenery and wildlife around me.

The first time out, I successfully left the driveway and headed down the block. I pulled in the clutch, made sure the bike was punched down into first gear with my left foot, signalled a right turn with my left hand, applied the brake with my right hand, and made a perfect stop at the corner. Sweet success!

Next I looked in both directions to ensure no one was coming, turned the handle bars toward the right, released the brake, and rolled on the throttle with my right hand to rev the engine. I then slowly let out the clutch lever with my left hand in order for the bike to engage and start moving forward. Check. Check. Check.

This was to be my first turn around the block and I was confident the bike would head in the right direction, however, instead of the bike turning sharply to the right as I envisioned, I ended up across the road on a neighbour's front lawn. In panic mode, I grabbed both the brakes and throttle at the same time which created a piercingly loud revving roar while the bike was standing still. I was terrified and before I knew it, I found myself on uneven ground and was unable to keep the bike upright. In extremely slow motion, the bike and I fell over on the grass. The bike was still running.

Peter dashed over to help. With an I-can't-believe-you-just-did-that look he asked me, "Why didn't you turn the bike?"

Frankly, I didn't know how to. My expectation and my experience didn't match up. Turning a motorcycle is very different than turning a car. You need to put strength and body into the bike to steer the bike in the right direction. I believe I may have given him a look back that said, "Never mind—just get this bike off me!"

That was only the beginning of a long learning process for me. The next question I had for my husband was, "How do I put the bike into second gear again?"

Before I could ride a bike competently, I had to do the work. I couldn't expect to be successful just because I sat on the bike. But I persevered, Peter persevered, and the licensing examiner, Tom, persevered, until that glorious moment two years later when I was granted a full Class 6 license.

When I rolled into the driveway afterward, I was met by my husband and my granddaughter Zoe. Big smiles on their faces, they held up signs congratulating me. They knew, as I did, what it took to get me there. We had plenty to celebrate.

This is a picture of what I hope to experience when Jesus returns. All those whom I have loved and have gone to Heaven before me will meet me there ready to celebrate with me. The picture would have been quite different if I had gotten complacent and stopped trying to learn and improve my riding skills. The examiner may never have given me my license.

In "The Parable of the Ten Virgins," success only happens for five of the ten women. Only five persevered by doing what was necessary to be ready for the arrival of the Bridegroom. All ten had the desire—but desire was not enough. Five women failed to be prudent and do what was necessary to be prepared. They found themselves separated from the Bridegroom. The loss must have been tremendously disappointing. They had devoted themselves to the Bridegroom. They had waited patiently for Him, yet when the time came, they were not ready and able to go.

It would be a feeling similar to having done everything possible to be ready for a wonderful holiday cruise with your family. For a year you saved, shopped, packed, counted down the days, and made plans with the family, but upon arriving at the dock, you see the ship sailing away without you. How could you have failed in the most important requirement of getting to the ship on time? You're devastated. It's not the way you planned it.

Now, let's imagine what it would be like if we were one of the five bridesmaids who were ready. We took the responsibility of getting extra oil seriously and did what it took prior to the arrival of the Bridegroom.

I can only imagine how fantastic an experience it would be to have my lamp burning brightly as the Bridegroom arrives to take me into the wedding banquet. With great joy we dance down the street to the party.

The gates swing open wide and the Bridegroom takes my hand and leads me into a stunningly beautiful banquet room adorned with the finest marble, gold, and sparkling gemstones. The family spared no expense! There are elaborate table decorations sitting on fine linen tablecloths with colours so vibrant it takes my breath away. The banquet is served with the finest of cuisine and wine of the best vintage. Our family and friends are singing, dancing, feasting, and laughing with one another. The women are dressed in beautiful fancy gowns and the men in tux and tails. The highest of standards are met in every aspect.

With love, the Bridegroom seats me in the most prominent, most comfortable chair at the banqueting table. He bends low to look into my eyes and smiles while asking me, "How may I serve you?" I feel His warmth and sincerity as I consider His request. Every desire that comes to my mind is filled to saturation. My greatest desire is to praise Him and give Him all the glory and honour He is due.

Yet that is only a picture of what will happen when Jesus, our Bridegroom, comes and welcomes those of us who are ready, through the gates of Heaven. When you think of Heaven, what comes to mind? Have you been taken in by a cream cheese commercial that paints a concept of Heaven? Drifting on white clouds, eating tasty snacks with your friends, while playing a lovely tune on a harp—boring!

Do you think that we will see and recognize all of our loved ones who have passed on before us? Will they be lined up inside the gate ready to greet us like a grand reception?

Do you see it as a place where almost everyone will go? Maybe you have an idea or standard in mind that would include or disqualify people based on how good or how bad they are.

Jesus shared many parables regarding the nature of the kingdom of Heaven. He warned that there will be a time of judgement in which some will qualify to enter in and others will not, as described in the following verses:

### Matthew 13:49-50

[49] *This is how it will be at the end of the age. The angels will come and separate the wicked from the righteous* [50] *and throw them into the blazing furnace, where there will be weeping and gnashing of teeth.*

He kept restating this warning because His desire is that none should perish. He quoted Old Testament scripture to warn that we need to be people who have eyes to see and ears to hear what He is teaching:

### Matthew 13:15-17

[15] *'For this people's heart has become calloused;*

*they hardly hear with their ears,*

*and they have closed their eyes.*

*Otherwise they might see with their eyes,*

*hear with their ears,*

*understand with their hearts*

*and turn, and I would heal them.'*

[16] *But blessed are your eyes because they see, and your ears because they hear.* [17] *For truly I tell you, many prophets and righteous people longed to see*

*what you see but did not see it, and to hear what you
hear but did not hear it.*

What Jesus really wants us to see, hear, and understand
is the great value of being one of God's treasures, as well as
the tragic consequences of choosing not to be one.

In the book of Revelation, we are reminded about being
blessed to be invited to the wedding supper which is to be
in Heaven:

### Revelation 19:9

[9] *Then the angel said to me, "Write this: Blessed are
those who are invited to the wedding supper of the
Lamb!" And he added, "These are the true words of
God."*

We are also given a description of what Heaven will be
like and reminded the time will be coming soon:

### Revelation 22:1-7

[1] *Then the angel showed me the river of the water of
life, as clear as crystal, flowing from the throne of God
and of the Lamb* [2] *down the middle of the great street*

*of the city. On each side of the river stood the tree of life, bearing twelve crops of fruit, yielding its fruit every month. And the leaves of the tree are for the healing of the nations. ³ No longer will there be any curse. The throne of God and of the Lamb will be in the city, and his servants will serve him. ⁴ They will see his face, and his name will be on their foreheads. ⁵ There will be no more night. They will not need the light of a lamp or the light of the sun, for the Lord God will give them light. And they will reign for ever and ever.*

*⁶ The angel said to me, "These words are trust-worthy and true. The Lord, the God who inspires the prophets, sent his angel to show his servants the things that must soon take place."*

*⁷ "Look, I am coming soon! Blessed is the one who keeps the words of the prophecy written in this scroll."*

Does Heaven hold an appeal to you? Does your desire to be in Heaven cause you to want to do whatever it takes to be ready? The good news is it's not too late but we don't know how much time we have left. We need the warning in Jesus' parable. We need to examine our lives and make sure we are doing what is necessary to be ready.

## CHAPTER SEVEN

# Sharing the Experience

A s I mentioned in the first chapter, while this book is primarily addressed to women, Jesus has a message for men about being ready as well. Despite what some might believe, men are not "born ready." It has been my experience that although men generally seem more comfortable learning how to ride a motorcycle than women, they still need to follow the same ground rules and have a plan for success.

My husband is always willing to provide coaching on the requirements of the motorcycle Skills Test. His personal experience in getting his licence, along with the experience he had in training me, attending multiple Skills Tests with me, and the perseverance to see me through it, helped to give him an understanding of what is required.

He states that it is vital that the student remains teachable. If I had become prideful and decided that I could learn on my own, I might never have discovered the bad habits I had formed. As well, I may have decided it was an impossible feat, sold the bike, and given up, making it look like that was the choice I wanted to make.

I know that there are many men who either succeed or fail based on their abilities but refuse help due to pride. There are also those who would rather sell their bike and claim it was for a reason other than their lack of skill or experience.

Let's examine again the warning Jesus gives to the men in the following parable:

### Luke 12:35-40

*[35] Be dressed ready for service and keep your lamps burning, [36] like servants waiting for their master to return from a wedding banquet, so that when he comes and knocks they can immediately open the door for him. [37] It will be good for those servants whose master finds them watching when he comes.*

*Truly I tell you, he will dress himself to serve, will have them recline at the table and will come and wait on them. [38] It will be good for those servants whose master finds them ready, even if he comes in the middle of the night or toward daybreak. [39] But understand this: If the owner of the house had known at what hour the thief was coming, he would not have let his house be broken into. [40] You also must be ready, because the Son of Man will come at an hour when you do not expect him."*

The literal context of this parable offers us a similar picture to what we read about Jesus' ministry where He often turned the tables on His disciples. When they expected Him to act the part of a King or a Conqueror, He often played the part of a servant. Instead of having His feet washed, He would wash the feet of His disciples.

I heard a sermon in which the pastor was painting a word-picture about what it will be like in Heaven. In his description he said that sometimes men have the wrong impression about Jesus. When asked why he thought many Christian men didn't attend church, he said it was because men have difficultly relating to a Jesus they could beat up! The Jesus on earth came as a Lamb to be sacrificed.

The Jesus who came to earth and submitted Himself to be the sacrifice for the sins of mankind required more courage than we could ever fully comprehend. Jesus came as a humble servant in order to show men how they ought to live in this lifetime. Just as described in the parable, we are all like servants waiting for the Master's return.

Men seem to forget that the same Jesus who was crucified is also the same Jesus who was brought back to life and rose to His proper place in Heaven. He is now the King of Kings seated on the throne of Heaven ruling over Heaven and earth and over all of creation. Jesus will never take a beating again. That was a one shot deal. All worship, glory, and honour belong to Him. Yet we see in this parable that Jesus, as Master, wants to show His love by turning the tables and serving His servants.

Jesus is not only our Bridegroom—He is also our Master! Our Conqueror! Our Defender and Protector! Powerful, the Lord of all! He is going to take down all His enemies and usher in the new kingdom. All the armies of Heaven are with Him. He will be seated on the throne giving final judgement on those who rejected Him. The punishment in hell will fit the crime and Jesus will be in authority to make it happen.

Men, don't let the Master (Jesus) return to find you asleep! He has an expectation to find you ready and waiting for Him. Don't let Him down; He's depending on you.

## CHAPTER EIGHT

# Reliving the Dream

What did I gain in learning to ride a motorcycle? I learned I can do all things through Christ who strengthens me. Seriously, there were a few times when I was ready to give up the challenge of learning. There were a few times when I would have given up trying to apply for the Class 6 license. There were even a few times when I would have dearly loved to have said to my husband, "You go ahead and ride—I'm going to take the easy road and stay home!" Instead, I felt challenged and excited when he said, "I can't believe you are really, seriously, contemplating learning to ride! You'd be willing to learn? Really?" He was proud of me and happy because I was willing to do something in which he felt pleasure.

I naively stepped up to the challenge and began the long, complicated, and arduous task of turning safe, careful Grandma into a "GRAMAHA." This is the affectionate term we have used since we purchased my 2005 Yamaha FZ6 sport bike. Yamaha's television and magazine advertisements would raise the question, "What kind of Yamaha are you?" and I would respond, "I'm a GRAMAHA!" (This is even engraved into my clutch lever).

The experience challenged the core of my being. I had to ask myself some serious questions, such as, "Is it worth the time, effort, and stress?" and "Is it worth the risk of injury and possibly death?"

My answer is a resounding YES! In spite of the difficulties, I persevered.

There is a verse in the Bible that encourages us to persevere, to run the race:

**Hebrews 12:1-3**
[1] *Therefore, since we are surrounded by such a great cloud of witnesses, let us throw off everything that hinders and the sin that so easily entangles. And let us run with perseverance the race marked out for us,* [2] *fixing our eyes on Jesus, the pioneer and per-*

*fecter of faith. For the joy set before him he endured the cross, scorning its shame, and sat down at the right hand of the throne of God. ³ Consider him who endured such opposition from sinners, so that you will not grow weary and lose heart.*

The Lord led me through each step, never giving me more than I could handle. If I'd had the full picture at the beginning, I may not have had the courage to see it through.

**Step One**: He put a desire in my heart. As I was walking past the flower shop, He brought my attention to a poster advertising a new ministry in town and in His still small voice He suggested this might be a ministry from which my husband would get pleasure.

**Step Two**: He put the desire in my heart to learn to ride on my own. As I was riding as a passenger, He gently suggested to me I should learn how to ride just in case something happened to us on the road and I needed to get help. Besides, I was getting a little bored not having anything to do but look right or left. He saw me through the challenges of learning, training, and gaining experience in riding. Now my husband and I truly enjoy a fantastic relationship by getting away on our bikes for an afternoon or a weekend or even a week-long holiday. We plan trips through spectacular scenery on smoothly paved winding back roads. We stay in hotels or bed and breakfast establishments that are dry, clean, and comfortable. We share memories of special experiences and encounters we have had along the way.

**Step Three**: He turned my heart toward those who did not yet know Him through the ministry of the Christian Motorcycle Association. I received prayer and evangelism training through their programs. I ride with the hope that Christ will use me wherever I am for His kingdom purposes. We have opportunities to meet new people and share the love of Jesus with them. We have served at motorcycle rallies and events, and have even spoken with people on the road, allowing us to shine the light of Jesus for others to see.

Running parallel to this time in my life, the Lord was also warming my heart toward Christian women who are struggling to keep their light shining for the Lord. He directed my thoughts toward "The Parable of the Ten Virgins." When I first read this parable, it caught hold of my heart. I wanted to know what Jesus meant about being ready and I wanted to know His expectation of us.

I asked other Christians what they believed it meant. I wanted to find out what pastors or seminary teachers believed the extra oil represented. The answers were found through the leading of the Holy Spirit as I began to write. He led me to look for answers in the Bible. He led me to answers through other Christians. He led me through showing me how my experiences matched His will. And as I wrote, He directed me step by step toward understanding as He revealed His truths.

I pray I have captured all He wants you to hear and have not added anything that would steer you away from His plans and purposes for your life. I also pray you will seek the Lord for more answers, greater understanding, and the help you need in order to be ready for His return. I, for one, do not want to be left standing outside the door of the banquet room because I have not done what is good and pleasing to God, and I pray the same goes for you.

### *Hebrews 12:14-15, 25-26, 28*

*[14] Make every effort to live in peace with everyone and to be holy; without holiness no one will see the Lord. [15] See to it that no one falls short of the grace of God and that no bitter root grows up to cause trouble and defile many.*

*[25] See to it that you do not refuse him who speaks. If they did not escape when they refused him who warned them on earth, how much less will we, if we turn away from him who warns us from heaven? [26] At that time his voice shook the earth, but now he has promised, "Once more I will shake not only the earth but also the heavens."*

*[28] Therefore, since we are receiving a kingdom that cannot be shaken, let us be thankful, and so worship God acceptably with reverence and awe ….*

As we look at the parables together, we find that Jesus wants to catch our attention. He wants us to be ready for His imminent return. It is His desire that none should perish, but that all would have everlasting life. The following passage from 2 Peter sums it up nicely:

**2 Peter 3:8-14**

*[8] But do not forget this one thing, dear friends: With the Lord a day is like a thousand years, and a thousand years are like a day. [9] The Lord is not slow in keeping his promise, as some understand slowness.*

*Instead he is patient with you, not wanting anyone to perish, but everyone to come to repentance.*

*[10] But the day of the Lord will come like a thief. The heavens will disappear with a roar; the elements will be destroyed by fire, and the earth and everything done in it will be laid bare.*

*[11] Since everything will be destroyed in this way, what kind of people ought you to be? You ought to live holy and godly lives [12] as you look forward to the day of God and speed its coming. That day will bring about the destruction of the heavens by fire, and the elements will melt in the heat. [13] But in keeping with his promise we are looking forward to a new heaven and a new earth, where righteousness dwells.*

*[14] So then, dear friends, since you are looking forward to this, make every effort to be found spotless, blameless and at peace with him.*

The parables are a great reminder that the time is coming when the Lord will return. There are more and more signs pointing to that fact. Even as I write this book I wonder if I have enough time to get it published before He comes again.

Let's not become complacent.

Let's not put off until tomorrow what we can do for the Lord today.

But, instead, let's get ready for when the Lord returns …

… Maranatha—come Lord Jesus, come!

Peter with CMA members Rick and Jean

Linda and her training bike
1983 Honda Interceptor

Zoe sporting t-shirt
"My Granny can whoop your Fanny"

Linda with her 2005 Yamaha FZ6

Linda on Old Hedley Road near Princeton, BC

CMA Rally Ride at 100 Mile House, BC

Peter at vacation cabin in Cherryville, BC

Linda and Peter on Road Trip in British Columbia

Vacation at Tibbles Lake, BC